<table>
<tr><td>

CONDITIONING EXERCISES

for

BEGINNERS

and

ADVANCED HARPISTS

as well as for

TOURING HARPISTS

by

</td><td>

EXERCICES D'ASSOUPLISSEMENT

pour

HARPISTES COMMENCANTS

et

AVANCES

ainsi que pour

HARPISTES EN TOURNEES

par

</td></tr>
</table>

CARLOS SALZEDO

These exercises should be practiced in various degrees of speed and strength, with an irreproachable position and the fullest action of the fingers.

It is not essential to practice them exclusively in C major. Their technical value will not be impaired if they are practiced with different pedal combinations, and their musical interest will be extended. For example, in the first six exercises, one can set pedals E♭, A♭ and B♭ (Æolian mode — usually referred to as "normal" or "natural" minor), or E♭ and A♭ (harmonic minor), or E♭ going up and B♭, A♭, E♭ going down (melodic minor). In exercises VII and VIII, one will obtain a great variety by using D♭, or D♯, or B♭ and D♭, or B♭, D♭ and F♯, or any combination resulting from mixing sharps with flats and naturals.

When played with the left hand, these exercises will be transposed an octave lower.

SPECIAL NOTE FOR TOURING HARPISTS

The touring harpist does not always have the opportunity to practice but can only warm up his fingers and limber up his muscles. He will find it more beneficial to play all these exercises without intermission one after the other, first with the right hand, then with the left (or vice versa) instead of alternating the hands after each exercise. The playing time of these exercises —for each hand—is approximately from 8 to 12 minutes, depending on the tempo; for example: ♩ = 40, 12 minutes 25 seconds; ♩ = 50, 10 minutes, 10 seconds; ♩ = 60, 8 minutes, 35 seconds (condensed version not included).

On devra travailler ces exercices dans différents degrés de force et de vitesse, avec une position irréprochable et l'action la plus complète des doigts.

Il n'est pas essentiel de les travailler exclusivement en Do majeur. Leur valeur technique ne sera pas amoindrie si on les travaille avec les pédales disposées de différentes manières, et l'intérêt musical ne fera qu'y gagner. Par exemple, dans les six premiers exercices, on pourra employer les pédales Mi♭, La♭ et Si♭ (mode éolien), ou Mi♭ et La♭ (harmonique mineur), ou Mi♭ en montant et Si♭, La♭, Mi♭ en descendant (mélodique mineur). Dans les exercices VII et VIII, on obtiendra une grande variété en employant Ré ♭, ou Ré ♯, ou Si ♭ et Ré ♭, ou Si ♭, Ré ♭ et Fa ♯, ou toute autre combinaison obtenue en mélangeant dièses, bémols et bécarres.

Lorsque joués de la main gauche, ces exercices devront être tranposés une octave plus bas.

NOTE SPÉCIALE POUR HARPISTES EN TOURNÉE

En tournée, le harpiste n'a pas toujours le loisir de travailler mais seulement de se dégourdir les doigts et d'assouplir ses muscles. Il obtiendra un meilleur résultat en jouant tous ces exercices sans interruption l'un après l'autre, la main droite d'abord, la main gauche ensuite (ou vice versa) au lieu d'alterner les mains après chaque exercice. L'exécution de ces exercices—pour chaque main—est approximativement de 8 à 12 minutes suivant les mouvements pris; par exemple: ♩ = 40, 12 minutes 25 secondes; ♩ = 50, 10 minutes 10 secondes; ♩ = 60, 8 minutes 35 seconds (version condensée non comprise).

RIGHT HAND

MAIN DROITE

I

43375

II

Place only one finger in advance
Ne placer qu'un doigt en avance

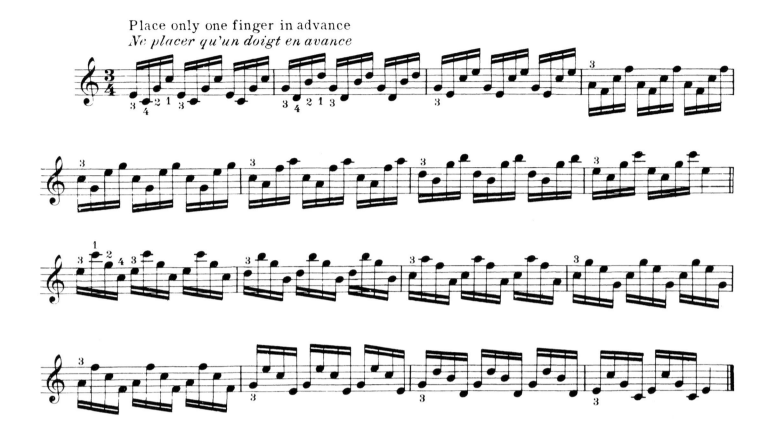

III

Place only one finger in advance
Ne placer qu'un doigt en avance

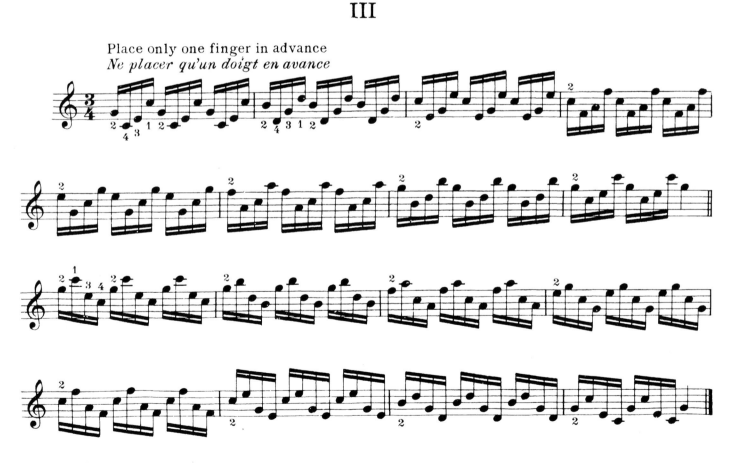

IV

In the three following exercises, play each chord rigorously unbroken.   These three exercises should be also practiced arpeggioed with strong accent on the thumb and second finger (observing strictly all placings in order to develop strength in those two fingers.

Dans les trois exercices qui suivent, jouer chaque accord rigoureusement plaqué.   Ces trois exercices devront être aussi travaillé arpégé en accentuant fortement le pouce et le deuxième doigt (observant strictement tous les placés) afin de développer la force dans ces deux doigts.

43375

8

VII

VIII

43375

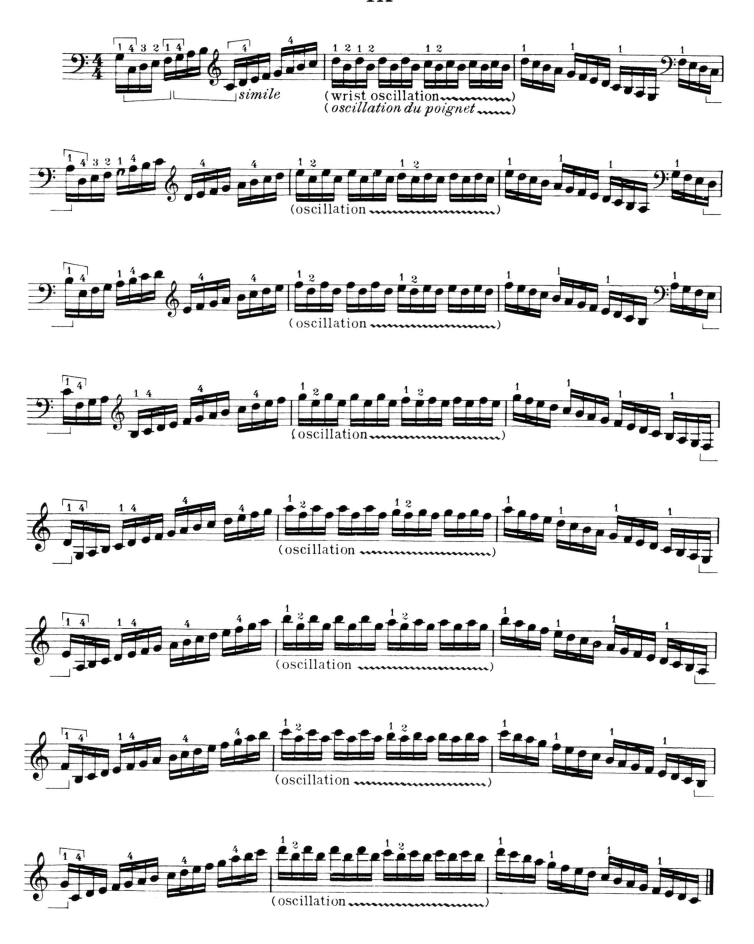

X

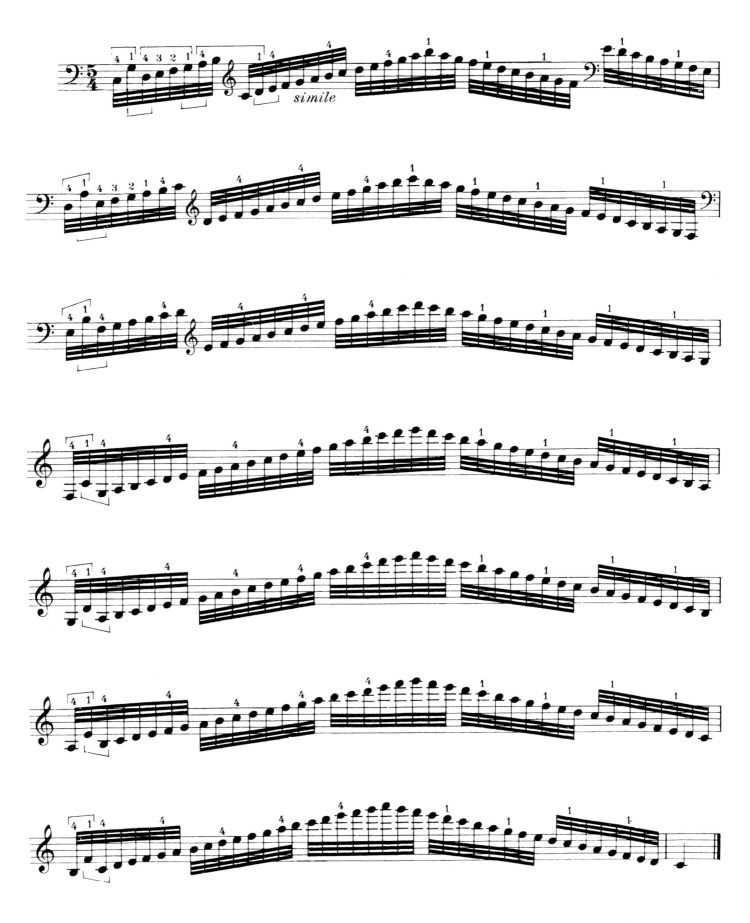

CONDENSED VERSION
OF THE FIRST SIX EXERCISES

VERSION CONDENSÉE
DES SIX PREMIERS EXERCICES

Place only one finger in advance
Ne placer qu'un doigt en avance

Play each chord rigorously unbroken
Jouer chaque accord rigoureusement plaqué

November 10, 1951
Fort Lauderdale, Florida

43375

METHOD FOR THE HARP by CARLOS SALZEDO
In collaboration with LUCILE LAWRENCE

This work contains fundamental exercises with illustrations and technical explanations, serving as an introduction and complement to Carlos Salzedo's "Modern Study of the Harp." In addition, this method contains fifteen Preludes for beginners, each of which has been purposely written in a different key in order that the beginner may become familiar with the manner of key formation on the harp.

In these Preludes, the pedals have been used extensively to avoid harmonic monotony as well as to give beginners the opportunity of becoming acquainted at once with the use of the pedals.

THE ABC OF HARP PLAYING by LUCILE LAWRENCE

The book consists of two sections. Part I (six chapters) contains studies and pieces, designed to introduce the beginner to the use of the pedals, the reading of notes and the finding of corresponding strings on the instrument. Part II is devoted to the use of the harp in the orchestra and deals with such problems as the tuning and regulating of the harp, fingering and flux, (formerly called "glissandi"). It contains many examples of orchestra writing and adaptations of examples to the harp.

An indispensable method for beginners as well as advanced players, orchestrators and arrangers.

THE HARPIST'S DAILY DOZEN by CARLOS SALZEDO

"The Harpist's Daily Dozen" can be used by all harpists with the exception of beginners. Its aim is to allow busy or touring harpists to keep up their technique with the minimum of effort.

As in the "Method for the Harp" and the "Modern Study of the Harp," both hands are developed to the same degree of efficiency, and the text appears in English and French.

Technical explanations in the introduction will assist the artist in obtaining full value in a limited practice period.

MODERN STUDY OF THE HARP by CARLOS SALZEDO

These Studies are not addressed solely to harpists, but to all who are interested in every musical manifestation. Composers and conductors alike will find in them information which will confirm their intuitions or solve their doubts, both with respect to the notation and the innumerable resources of the harp of to-day.

Novices as well as virtuosi can profit by these Studies.

Technically, they will develop (in the same degree for both hands) a logical knowledge of fingering and of the various tone-effects.

THE ART OF MODULATING by CARLOS SALZEDO
In collaboration with LUCILE LAWRENCE

This book, primarily intended for harpists, is also adaptable to the need of organists and pianists. It contains practical modulating formulas, examples of modulations, extensions, cadenzas, and a complete illustration of harmonic fluxes (formerly called "glissandi"). Because this treatise was prepared mainly for the use of instrumentalists with but a slight knowledge of harmony, ninth chords, suspensions, and other elaborate harmonic devices have not been used in the modulating formulas.

In addition, the work contains ten fragments of dances and five easy characteristic pieces for the harp.
The text apears in English and French.

CONDITIONING EXERCISES by CARLOS SALZEDO

The touring harpist does not always have the opportunity to practice but can only warm up his fingers and limber up his muscles. He will find it more beneficial to play all these exercises without intermission one after the other, first with the right hand, then with the left (or vice versa) instead of alternating the hands after each exercise. The playing time of these exercises — for each hand — is approximately from 8 to 12 minutes, depending on the tempo; for example: = 40, minutes 25 seconds; = 50, 10 minutes, 10 seconds; = 60, 8 minutes, 35 seconds (condensed version not included).

0 73999 86820 3

HL50286820

G. SCHIRMER, Inc.
DISTRIBUTED BY
HAL•LEONARD®
CORPORATION
7777 W. BLUEMOUND RD. P.O. BOX 13819 MILWAUKEE, WI 53213

ISBN-13: 978-0-7935-5539-0

Distributed By
HAL LEONARD

50286820

9 780793 555390

U.S. $7.